The Essential

COLLEGE

ADMISSIONS

HANDBOOK

YOUR STRESS-FREE PATH TO COLLEGE ACCEPTANCES

LISA GUSS & SHARI KRAMER

TABLE OF CONTENTS

INTRODUCTION

How to Navigate the Competitive World of College Admissions

The college admissions process can be stressful, overwhelming, and cumbersome. Where do I start? What needs to get done? How do I know what colleges are good for me? How can I stand out from other applicants? And how can I keep my sanity? Today's admissions environment is more competitive than ever, and guidance counselors carry ever-increasing workloads. This leaves parents and students wondering how to begin on the path toward college acceptances.

We are here to help! *THE ESSENTIAL COLLEGE ADMISSIONS HANDBOOK* offers clear and practical advice to guide you through the competitive and complex world of college admissions. With more than 25 years of combined experience in the college admissions field, we have worked with hundreds of families to effectively break down this intimidating process into manageable and well-organized steps. Our philosophy is simple: to help you through each critical piece of the college process, while maintaining a sense of humor and harmony at home. Our step-by-step approach will enable you to stay focused, motivated, and on track to meet your goals. The result? Anxiety is reduced, milestones are met, and applications are cohesive and reflect your unique story.

By following our guidelines, you will find colleges that are best suited to meet your individual needs; colleges that will provide an environment that fosters your educational, social, and personal growth. Start thinking about where you see your future. Get to know yourself and discover your passions and what excites you academically. Be proactive and own the process. This is an exciting time, so enjoy the journey and celebrate your accomplishments. Don't procrastinate or allow stress to hinder your progress. You've already taken the first step by starting this book! Now, take a deep breath and read on.

From early planning as a high school freshman to college acceptances as a senior, *THE ESSENTIAL COLLEGE ADMISSIONS HANDBOOK* will help you navigate every critical step in the admissions process! Each chapter will provide you with vital information about the various components of the college admissions process. And at the end of each chapter, you will find homework for yourself and your parents; homework that will keep you focused and on course.

The unknown is scary, but this process doesn't have to be. Invest the time, read carefully, and do your homework. When you do, you will reduce the mystique and stress surrounding the college process. And you will find the success you deserve—acceptance letters from colleges where you feel at home, where you will grow, and where you can thrive.

1. EARLY PLANNING

Calling All Freshmen and Sophomores to the Starting Line

It's okay if you didn't start planning for college in kindergarten! You are not behind if your childhood Legos and blocks didn't spell out the SAT Word of the Day! We believe in early planning, but within reason. As a freshman or sophomore in high school, you are in the ideal position to start educating yourself about college admissions and learning the critical milestones that you should achieve over the next four years. The college admissions process is just that, a process. And it includes a series of steps and actions. It can be overwhelming to navigate, so move forward slowly and sensibly. Keep in mind that the path isn't always smooth and straight. There may be twists and turns along the way. But by pushing forward, your journey will conclude with college acceptances and celebrations!

Freshman and sophomore years of high school are the time to think about the big picture (we will focus on the details in later chapters where strategies and activities specific to the juniors and seniors are highlighted). Start by assessing where you currently are in the college process. Does the word *college* dominate every family dinner conversation? Are you frustrated that you don't have a career path already mapped out? Are you annoyed when compared to your older brother, your older cousin, or your mother's friend's niece's best friend? If you answered *Yes* to any of these questions, then it's time to hit pause, and add a little fun to the process.

Think about what makes you happy. Think about what you want to do when you *grow up*. And think about what and how you like to learn. Don't put undue pressure on yourself to answer these questions in great detail; just reflect! You don't want to burn out freshman year! By setting realistic expectations and goals for the next four years, you will manage the process and therefore, manage the stress.

For now, let's stay focused on three things that are important for high school freshmen and sophomores: extracurricular activities (clubs, community service, jobs), high school course selection, and developing relationships with teachers and guidance counselors.

EXTRACURRICULAR ACTIVITIES

Extracurricular activities can be quite varied, and they include jobs, clubs, and community service/volunteering. Your long-term goal should be involvement in activities that are meaningful to you and that reflect what is important to you. However, at this early stage, we encourage you to try a variety of activities. This is the time to focus on the breadth of activities, not your depth of interest. We will discuss how to delve into each type of activity in *Chapter 3*. Freshman and sophomore years should be times of exploration; see what activities you like and what sparks your passion. Try the Environmental Club and go to a few meetings and events. Not for you? It's okay! Try the Spanish Club and help with a fundraiser. Not feeling the connection and not understanding one word? It's okay! But don't give up.

As a high school student, it is essential to be involved in both your school and your community. Think about what you like to do and what activities involve or complement those interests. Opportunities are endless. Some are just more obvious than others. Some clubs are hands-on, some are academic, and some are service-driven. Find what works for you. And keep in mind that you don't need to be constrained by what is already organized. Do you wish there was a club that involved helping local senior citizens or one that raised money for the animal shelter? If you feel that way, chances are other students do, too. Talk to a teacher and start a club. You will be engaged, enthusiastic, and you will demonstrate leadership skills. Above all, you will spend time doing something that matters to you!

Remember, every activity and every job is important. They all count and all demonstrate key character strengths that colleges look favorably upon. If you are the kid who can cure a rare disease, that's awesome; but if you are like most high school students, this is a bit out of reach. Try to make a difference on a smaller scale. Clean up your streets and parks on Earth Day. Collect clothing for your local homeless shelter. Just be you. College admissions officers realize that you are a teenager with young adult interests, skills, and accomplishments. Everything you do matters. For example, babysitting shows responsibility, kindheartedness, and a strong work ethic. Mowing lawns and shoveling driveways show an entrepreneurial spirit. Helping your church or synagogue youth group stock a food pantry demonstrates compassion and commitment to helping others. Get creative, get moving, and get involved!

It's important to keep track of all your extracurricular activities starting with freshman year. Otherwise, you risk forgetting all the ways you were involved. Keeping track as you go along will also make filling out college applications much easier down the road! Think about the following: What activities am I doing? What is my specific role within these activities? Do I have leadership responsibilities? How many hours do I spend on each activity and how many weeks per year am I involved? Write everything down! Also, save any articles that relate to your activities. Keep a folder in a central place, like your night table or your kitchen island, and add things to the folder as you accomplish them. Don't worry about wording at this point. You can fix grammar and spelling later on. For now, just get your list of activities down on paper.

COURSE SELECTION

If you have researched the college process, then you have seen the word *rigor* over and over again. Quite simply, colleges want you to challenge yourself. Admissions officers are aware of what your high school offers, and they want you to take full advantage of advanced classes. However, we want to remind you about the importance of maintaining a healthy balance. What makes sense for you? Absolutely push yourself academically and realize your potential, but also recognize your limits. Don't take on more than you can handle. Take some time to reflect on your personal goals. Then stay true to yourself and what is important to you!

If you are hoping to attend an Ivy League college, then you will want to fill your schedule with honors or AP classes as early as possible to lay the necessary foundation for your four years of high school. Set your academic goals and learn your high school's specific rules and pre-requisites for advanced classes. For instance, in many schools, in order to be on track to take calculus, you need to be in an accelerated math class as early as ninth grade.

If you are like most students whose goal is not an Ivy League college, you still need to plan, but you don't need to take every advanced class offered. Think about where your strengths and passions are and push yourself in those areas. For example, if you are thinking about pursuing engineering in college, then challenge yourself with advanced math classes. If you are interested in the health profession, then push yourself and consider doubling up on science classes. Straight *As* on your report card is awesome, but it might mean you didn't challenge yourself enough. Maybe you should consider moving up a level in one or two classes next year. Most colleges prefer a *B+* in an AP class to an *A* in a college prep class. Not everyone is an AP student, and that is fine. Just be honest with yourself about your goals and abilities. Know who you are, work hard, stay focused, and do your best.

Electives are an opportunity to explore your passions and perhaps discover some new ones. Read the course descriptions. Talk to other students. Try new classes. Don't worry if all of your classes are not exclusively academic. If you are interested in health, take a foods or nutrition class. If you are creative, consider photography or painting. If you love business, choose a class on financial literacy. This book is about college planning, but this process is about finding out who you are, where you will do well, and what makes you happy. Ultimately, finding answers to these questions will result in being successful as you embark on the next stage of life—college.

BUILDING RELATIONSHIPS WITH GUIDANCE COUNSELORS AND TEACHERS

For most college applications, you will need a recommendation letter from your guidance counselor and from one or two teachers. The strongest recommendations are the ones where it is apparent that the teacher knows you well, both academically and personally. It is never too early to start building these key relationships. We are sure that your guidance department is like most we have visited— understaffed and overworked. Guidance counselors tend to know the troublemakers in school or the students at the very top of the class. Most of you will not fall into either of these categories. You probably meet with guidance once a year to discuss classes. So, unless you make a concerted effort, this limited contact will not enable you to build a relationship that results in a genuine and convincing college recommendation. Fortunately, there is an easy fix. We are not advising you become a fixture in the guidance office, but you should make it your business to talk to your counselor a few times a year so that he/she can get to know you beyond your transcript. How can you do this? It's simple. If you are deciding between two classes to add to your schedule, ask your counselor for his/her recommendation. If you are having trouble in a class, ask your counselor for advice. If you are excited to start the college process, keep him/her in the loop with your progress. And if you happen to bake delicious cookies, a homemade holiday gift is always appreciated!

By spring of junior year, you should be prepared to ask two teachers for college recommendation letters. It is preferable if both recommendations are not from the same academic area. For example, try not to ask both your biology teacher and your chemistry teacher for recommendations. Focus on which teacher knows your strong work ethic or who understands how passionate you are about learning. It is not necessarily about the class where you got an A; it's the class where you demonstrated who you are as a student. Think about how you can foster these teacher relationships. Go for extra help when needed. Be prepared with questions and be specific with the help you need. This will show your teacher that you have worked through the material the best you can and now need his/her help to fully understand the information. Be an active class participant. Teachers appreciate students who contribute to class discussions and enhance the learning of fellow students. Always complete assignments fully and on-time, make up work from any absences, and be respectful in class. Put your phone away and give your teacher your complete attention.

OFF TO A GREAT START

It is early in the college process. Be proud of yourself for starting on the path toward college admissions. Knowledge is crucial to success. Stay focused on what is important to you and try to minimize the noise you will hear from friends and well-meaning family members. Keep your long-term goals in mind and pay attention to the areas you can work on now.

HOMEWORK FOR THE STUDENT:

- Why is college important to you?
- What are your long-term academic goals?
- Develop specific action items as they relate to the items in this chapter:
  o Identify three clubs or activities that you will explore.
  o Create an academic map to ensure you stay on target to meet your long-term goals.
  o Research two electives that may be interesting to you.
  o Increase your participation in class.

HOMEWORK FOR THE PARENT:

- Why do you want your child to attend college?
- What are your long-term objectives and academic goals for your child?
- What clubs or activities do you think might interest your child? Have an open discussion with him/her about these possibilities.
- Look at your school's academic offerings. Write down some classes you think might interest your child and discuss the options with him/her.
- Keep the discussions light. Don't overwhelm your child at this point. This is a long process, and you don't want unnecessary stress to interfere with progress. As we advised your child above, keep out the extraneous noise you will hear from friends. Focus on your child, not on what your co-workers, neighbors, or exercise partners say they are doing.

NOTES

NOTES

2. COURSE SELECTION

Physics, Algebra, or Study Hall

A re you taking mostly college prep classes? Or loading up on AP classes? Or are you the student constantly searching for the No Homework classes? If you are in that last category, then it is time for a wake-up call. As we discussed in *Chapter 1—Early Planning*, course selection is an integral part of the college admissions process. Colleges want well-rounded students who have challenged themselves throughout high school. They look at what your high school offers and whether you are taking advantage of these opportunities. Be honest with yourself. Have you challenged yourself and shown increasing rigor over your four years of high school? Or did you take Anatomy over Physics because your best friend did or because you felt it was easier? Sometimes that's okay, but more often than not, it isn't. Every component of your application is part of your story; and it should be a truthful, compelling, and consistent story. The academic piece of your story will be shown on your transcript. Increasing the rigor of your course load each year will demonstrate your work ethic, your ability to manage time effectively, your desire to learn, and most importantly, the foundation you are laying for your future and the type of college student you will be.

The goal for every student is simple. Strive for the best grades in the most challenging courses that are appropriate for you. A *B+* in Earth Science is impressive if you have done your best work, participated in extra help sessions, and put in the time and effort to study. If you are nodding your head in agreement because this sounds like you, then good work! However, if you didn't put much effort into that Earth Science grade, then you have just uncovered an opportunity—an opportunity to work harder and earn an *A* or an opportunity to move up a level and take a more advanced class next year. Take a look at your homework answers from *Chapter 1—Early Planning*. What are your goals for college, as well as your long-term academic goals? The answers to these questions will help you establish a path toward finding your best-fit college. And course selection is a central and significant stepping-stone on this path. Every student has his or her own path to success. Find the one that fits your goals and make sure you consistently work toward it.

Remember, you are not the same student as your older sister or your father's co-worker's son. You need to create your own academic story, and high school is just the beginning. Colleges assess the path you have taken so far and then make assumptions regarding what track you will follow in college. Will you take the paved and steady route? Will you push yourself and hike uphill? Or will your path descend to lower ground? Let your transcript tell your story, and let that story be positive, persuasive, and convincing. Each year, you should increase the rigor and level of your classes wherever possible. Take advantage of any new challenge!

HAVE YOU ALWAYS BEEN A HIGH ACHIEVER?

Some of you have taken advanced classes since middle school. You have always been focused and motivated. That's admirable; keep it going and continue this trend by working hard to get the best grades possible. But, don't stop there. It is still important to look for ways to increase your rigor every year. Look at the classes where you earned an *A*. Did this come easily? Do you have the opportunity to move up a level? Don't let fear get in your way. Colleges prefer that you challenge yourself and get a *B* in a higher-level class than be satisfied with an easy *A*. Look at it from their perspective. What does your chosen path show them about the student who will walk their campus? Students who consistently challenge themselves demonstrate motivation and a desire to learn. Pushing yourself academically is a character trait that colleges value.

ARE HONORS AND AP CLASSES NEW TO YOU?

Not everyone takes advanced classes early on. Some of you may have entered high school feeling a bit more apprehensive. The transition from middle school is not always easy, and your focus may have been on acclimating to the new social environment and not on academics. That's okay. There is still plenty of time to challenge yourself. It is never too late, and it is always important to look for ways to increase your rigor. Every student should have the same overall goal— the best grades in the most challenging (yet appropriate) courses. Can you add at least one advanced class? Can you push yourself a little bit out of your comfort zone? Don't be afraid of your first honors or AP class. If your teacher recommends you for the advanced level class, then go into it feeling confident and ready. Confidence is a building block to success. College admissions officers will notice an upward trajectory of grades and rigor. Their hope is this trend will continue in college. Most often, GPA and coursework rigor are the most important criteria for admissions.

DO YOUR CLASSES REFLECT YOUR PASSIONS?

Another important facet of course selection is passion. Everyone has a passion. Some find it earlier than others. If you don't think you have a passion, don't be overwhelmed by this word. Think of it this way. What are your interests? What do you enjoy? How do you like to spend your free time? What do you think about? Are you obsessed with video games? Do you love food? Are you a budding novelist? Or are you glued to HGTV? Let's translate these passions or interests into the electives you choose in high school. For the gamers, take a look at a computer science or computer applications class. For our foodies, perhaps you can take a culinary arts or nutrition class. Journalism or creative writing classes are ideal for our authors. And finally, if you are reading this with HGTV on in the background, turn off the TV and sign up for an interior design or architecture elective. What's our message? Don't make this complicated! Take classes you like whenever possible. When you care about the subject matter, you will be focused, you will work hard, and your grades will reflect your attention and effort. Electives are a chance for you to discover and demonstrate your passions. In *Chapter 3*, we will talk to you about activities. Ideally, your academic passions will align with your extracurricular activities and will add to the consistency and compelling nature of your application and your personal story.

MAKE GOOD CHOICES

Every year, your course selection is an opportunity to challenge yourself academically and to follow your interests and passions. Remember who you are and focus on your goals. Remember to keep out the noise and ignore the nosy neighbor talking about her nephew's seemingly stellar accomplishments. Your academic story should reflect your strengths, your commitment, and your interests. If you stay focused on this, your path will be well paved and will lead you to a happy and successful college experience.

HOMEWORK FOR THE STUDENT:

- Are you challenging yourself academically?
- Are you pursuing classes that interest you?
- Think about a few additional core classes that will add rigor to your schedule next year.
- Write down four of your interests and research your school's elective offerings to see what courses fit these interests.

HOMEWORK FOR THE PARENT:

- Do you see your child working hard to get the grades he/she is receiving?
- Is there an area in which he/she can challenge himself/herself more?
- Write down what interests your child outside of academics and compare these interests to your school offerings. Are there any electives you think fit your child interests?
- Have a discussion with your child about the material in this chapter and your answers to these homework questions.
- Help him/her develop the confidence needed to take on new challenges and to achieve success.

NOTES

NOTES

3. EXTRACURRICULAR ACTIVITIES

Put Down the Remote and Get Involved

Are you the youngest CEO of a tech startup? We aren't; we just figured out how to use Snapchat filters. Are you training for the Olympics? We aren't; we consider ourselves accomplished after a two-mile run. Are you writing a book uncovering the secret to achieving world peace? We aren't; we are merely hoping for peace in your home during the college admissions process! Chances are that you, as well as most of the admissions representatives reading your applications, are not involved in any of these activities. Most of you are *regular kids* who just need to focus on how you can be involved and make meaningful contributions to your school and community.

Admissions officers look at how potential students use their time outside of school and how it reveals important personal dimensions that statistics can't show. Extracurricular activities can be quite varied and include jobs, clubs, and community service and volunteering. In *Chapter 1—Early Planning*, we discussed identifying those activities that are interesting and meaningful to you. Moving forward, as you enter junior or senior year of high school, it's time to delve into your specific role in these activities.

To get started, think about why it is important to participate in extracurricular activities and what it conveys to admissions. Participating in an extracurricular activity (such as student government, a sport, a part-time job, or volunteering), while maintaining good grades, demonstrates many character strengths, including the following:

- **Time-Management Skills.** Colleges know that you have a lot on your plate and they will look to see how effectively you balance the varied components of your busy high school life. For example, a student-athlete spends hours training each day for the better part of the year. Colleges respect athletes who continue to thrive academically while showing commitment to their sport.

- **Ability to Prioritize**. What is important to you? Grades and schoolwork need to be at the top of your list, so keep in mind that it is better to do a few things well, than to overschedule yourself and have no true accomplishments to highlight. Colleges want students who pursue extracurricular activities while maintaining their strong academic story.

- **Motivation.** Your activities outside of the classroom show your willingness to be active, involved, and committed. Colleges look for students who will contribute to their campus and the local community. Students who have already demonstrated their desire to become involved in their school, their community, and within their circle of family and friends are more likely to do the same when they become part of a college community.

- **Responsibility**. Responsibility is a key indicator of success in college and beyond, and is demonstrated over time. Consistency is the key; so maintain your involvement during the school year, during the summer, and throughout high school. A job, a leadership position, and taking the initiative all demonstrate a student's ability to be a responsible member of a community.

- **Leadership Qualities**. As a junior or senior, this vital component of your story will differentiate you from other applicants. Some leadership positions may be obvious, such as student council officer, club president, or team captain; but there are other ways to demonstrate leadership, as well. Students who organize fundraisers, start entrepreneurial enterprises, or form new clubs all show important leadership characteristics.

CHOOSE DEPTH OVER BREADTH

Admission officers are more likely to consider an applicant who is deeply and passionately committed to a specific activity over a student who is superficially involved in multiple activities. This refinement process takes place over time. As we mentioned in *Chapter 1—Early Planning*, use your freshman and sophomore years to explore multiple and varied interests. Junior and senior years should be spent delving into those activities that interest you the most. You do not have to join every club at your school. Find one or two that interest you and get involved, really involved. Do more than attend meetings. Initiate and develop a new fundraiser. Get a position on the board. Write an article for your newspaper highlighting the club's mission, goals, and accomplishments. Choose depth over breadth.

CONSIDER INTERESTS AND ABILITIES

We've already discussed how your course selection, particularly your elective course selection, should be aligned with your interests and passions. Now let's take this same approach and think about how your clubs, jobs, or community service should correspond with and complement your interests, as well. By getting involved in activities that interest you, your passion will be evident! A student who is a talented writer should consider working on the school newspaper or yearbook. An animal lover should volunteer at a local shelter. Do not fill your list with activities that have no meaning to you. Think about what you identified as your interests in *Chapter 2—Course Selection.* Are you spending your time doing things that you love? College admissions officers are smart. They can differentiate between students who do community service solely for a *prestigious* entry on their resume and students who do it because they care. So, how is this accomplished? If you are the video game enthusiast, get a job in a video store or initiate a donation drive and collect video games for a local charity. If you are the foodie we referenced in *Chapter 2*, get a job at a restaurant or write a food blog. If you are our budding novelist, perhaps you can lead a book club at your local library or write an article for the community paper. And if you are our HGTV fan, take a summer class in interior design or shadow an architect or designer.

USE INTERNSHIPS TO DEVELOP INTERESTS

Internships and shadowing opportunities can help you pursue your passions, discover interesting and exciting activities, and learn about potential career paths. Work experience can also help you identify possible college majors or concentrations. Keep in mind that learning what you don't like is just as important as learning what you do like. Both positive and negative experiences help you hone in on your specific path.

SEEK A BALANCE

Achieve a balance between academics and extracurricular activities. Participating in too many activities can take away from study time. It can also lead to burnout, exhaustion, and unnecessary stress. Know your potential and know your limits. Remember that it's important to not only survive the college process, but also to thrive as you navigate the path that is right for you.

HOMEWORK FOR THE STUDENT:

- What extracurricular activities have you participated in since ninth grade?
- Capture the following pieces of information for each activity: description of the activity, your specific role, and approximate time spent (hours/week and weeks/year).
- Think about the activity or activities that interest you the most and brainstorm ideas to deepen your involvement and commitment to these activities.
- Develop a plan and timeline to implement these ideas.

HOMEWORK FOR THE PARENT:

- Help your child stay organized and capture details on his/her activities. Our suggestion: keep a folder in a central place—a night table or kitchen island. Add things to the folder as your child accomplishes them.
- Write down what seems to interest your child the most or what appears to spark his/her enthusiasm. Are there any clubs, jobs or community service opportunities you think might be a natural fit for your child?
- Have a discussion with your child about how to deepen his/her involvement in key activities.
- Help him/her to feel confident in order to take on new challenges and to set him/her up for success.

NOTES

NOTES

4. TESTING STRATEGIES

Sharpen Your #2 Pencil

SAT. ACT. SAT 2. SAT Subject Test. AP Exam. UGH!! The college process is filled with standardized tests. Junior year should be nicknamed Year of the Acronym! But take a breath. Don't think of the SAT as a Scholastic Aptitude Test; instead, take a moment to *Stop And Think*.

Will the sharpness of your #2 pencil determine your future? Will your hacking cough on test day determine your future? Will the decibel level of your rumbling stomach as the SAT begins determine your future? *No!* Your future will not be solely determined by the pattern of those little darkened circles on the scantron sheet! Standardized tests are just one component of the college admissions process. Your grades, essays, recommendations, and activities all come together to form your completed application, and will all be reviewed by college admissions officers. However, because standardized tests are important, we do encourage you to go into test day equipped with several sharpened #2 pencils, healthy and well-rested, and satisfied after a good breakfast! So, *Stop And Think*, and let's examine what you need to know about college testing.

SAT VS. ACT

To apply to college, most students will need to take either the SAT or the ACT. There are some schools that are test optional (meaning standardized tests are not required), and we will discuss that later in this chapter. Colleges do not have a preference regarding SAT vs. ACT; the decision is up to you. So, let's talk about the similarities and differences between these two tests.

- Both tests are used in college admissions decisions and for consideration of merit-based scholarships.

- Both tests have an optional Writing section. Some colleges require it as part of their application review, so we recommend taking at least one test with the Writing section.

- Neither test penalizes students for incorrect answers.

- The SAT includes five sections: Reading (65 minutes for 52 questions), Writing and Language (35 minutes for 44 questions), Math with No Calculator (25 minutes for 20 questions), Math with Calculator (55 minutes for 38 questions) and Optional Writing (50 minutes for one essay). Testing time, including breaks and optional Writing, is approximately four hours.

- The ACT includes five sections: English (45 minutes for 75 questions), Math (60 minutes for 60 questions), Reading (35 minutes for 40 questions), Science (35 minutes for 40 questions), and Optional Writing (40 minutes for one essay). Testing time, including breaks and optional Writing, is approximately five hours.

- The SAT Math section includes arithmetic, problem-solving & data analysis, algebra, geometry, pre-calculus, and trigonometry. Formulas are provided. The ACT Math section includes arithmetic, algebra, functions, geometry, and trigonometry. Formulas are not provided.

- The SAT restricts the use of calculators to some sections. Calculators are allowed for all Math sections of the ACT. The SAT allows graphing calculators, but the ACT does not.

- The SAT has five reading passages, while the ACT has four.

- The SAT is scored on a 1600-point scale.

- The ACT is scored on a scale of 1–36. Your composite score is the average of your scores on the four main sections of the exam, rounded to the nearest whole number.

- The SAT and ACT are redesigned periodically based on feedback from college and high school counselors. Please review all test updates and requirements.

So, are you more confused than before? And are you still unsure which test you should take or which one will be better for you? Many students simply start with one and see how they do. If you are comfortable with the test and happy with the results, then you can continue with that particular test. If not, consider taking the other test and evaluate which result is stronger. If this type of scenario doesn't work for you, then consider taking a diagnostic test to help you determine where you will be more successful. Many test prep organizations offer this free service, and it's a good way to decide how to proceed!

WHEN TO START AND HOW TO PREPARE

Students often ask us when to take their first SAT or ACT. Because Algebra 2 is included on the tests, most students should wait until the winter or spring of their junior year so that they have enough knowledge in this subject area. However, if you are on the *fast track* for math and took Algebra 2 during your sophomore year, then you can take the SAT or ACT earlier in your junior year.

Once you have determined which test is right and when to start, then the next question is *How should I prepare?* There are several options, and you need to determine which option works best for you (both financially and academically). Private tutors are the first option, but not always within budget. Many private tutors offer discounts for small groups, so if you have a friend or friends at a similar academic level, this is a good option, as well. Another alternative is a test prep class. These are offered at most tutoring centers. If you are self-motivated, then an online prep class/program is a great option, as well, and is usually a budget-friendly way to prepare for the tests. And finally, some students prepare on their own using test prep books. Whatever method you choose, take the preparation seriously. Your test results will be directly impacted by the amount of time and focus you spend on your preparation.

Now that you have thought about how to prepare for the tests, you need to think about how often to take them. Colleges like to see students who continually work to improve their academics, so we recommend taking the tests often enough so you have two acceptable scores to submit with your applications. This shows consistency and/or improvement and also demonstrates that you care enough about college to give up a few Saturdays! In most situations, you will realize your optimal test score by your third sitting. Evaluate what optimal means to you and how to communicate these results to the colleges on your list. This is where we will introduce two new powerful and often confusing terms, Score Choice and Super Score.

SCORE CHOICE

Score Choice enables you to choose which scores you send to each college. For the SAT and the ACT, you have the option to send your score reports, by test date, to any college you chose. So, if you went into one test with a miserable cold, don't worry! If it wasn't a good test day for you, you do not need to send this test report. Please recognize that while there are a few schools that may request all of your test reports, most only consider your highest score from one test date or your highest section scores from all test dates. So, review each of your college's admission requirements before proceeding with Score Choice.

SUPER SCORE

The Super Score option can change your 1100 SAT score to an 1170, and your 27 ACT score can now be reported as a 29. How? No need for superpowers! Super Score will take care of this transformation. The SAT Super Score is the sum of your highest Math and highest Evidence-Based Reading and Writing (referred to as Reading) scores. For example, if your January test score was 600 Math and 500 Reading for an 1100 score and your March test score was a 570 in Math and 570 in Reading, then your Super Score is 600 Math (from January) plus the 570 Reading (from March), resulting in your 1170 Super Score. Your ACT Super Score is the average of your highest Math, Science, Reading, and English section scores. As with our SAT example, the new average score may be calculated across two or more test dates. As with Score Choice, it is essential to review the testing policy at each college to help determine what composite score they will be reviewing.

TEST OPTIONAL

Earlier, we mentioned the concept of *test optional* schools. There are currently more than 1,000 schools in the United States that do not require test scores for admission into bachelor degree programs. School administrators at these test-optional schools are concerned with the overemphasis on standardized tests and prefer to rely on your transcript, activities, and recommendations when arriving at an admission decision. Unfortunately, you cannot count on all the schools on your final college list being test optional, so you should prepare for and take standardized tests! For a current list of test optional schools, go to *www.fairtest.org*.

SAT SUBJECT TESTS

SAT Subject Tests, once known as SAT 2s, are yet another test in the extensive standardized test category. Let's remember to *Stop And Think*. What are these tests and do I really need to take them? While we know you are hoping to hear *No*, our answer is *It depends*. Some colleges, particularly the most selective schools, require the SAT Subject Test scores for admission, often requesting up to three tests in different subject areas. Subject Tests will cover a single subject, such as math, biology, US history, or Spanish. Each test lasts one hour. Some colleges may also use strong Subject Test scores to award course credit and/or allow you to place out of introductory classes. You have the option, using Score Choice, to send your scores for any or all of the Subject Tests you take, regardless of test date.

ADVANCED PLACEMENT TESTS

Are you enrolled in Advanced Placement (AP) classes? The advanced rigor of this coursework will demonstrate your ability to challenge yourself and perform at the level of a college student. The corresponding exams are not required for college admissions. They may, however, be used to earn course credit and/or allow you to place out of introductory classes. We recommend taking the AP test for each AP class in which you are enrolled. As with the other tests, it is your decision what scores you submit.

STOP AND THINK

How can we sum up standardized tests for college admission? Sharpen your pencils and sharpen your focus. Know the test that works best for you. Do your homework and research what each school on your college list requires for admission. Stay balanced, motivated, and healthy. The Year of the Acronym is almost over! You will survive, and with all your hard work, you will thrive!

HOMEWORK FOR THE STUDENT:

- Look into taking an SAT/ACT diagnostic test.
- Begin preparing for your test of choice.
- Research schools on your initial college list to see what tests are required or recommended for admission.
- Develop a testing schedule that includes the various tests needed.

HOMEWORK FOR THE PARENT:

- Discuss with your child which tests he/she may need.
- Decide on a preparation method that works for you financially and fits your child's needs and timetable.
- Check in with your child on a regular basis to ensure that he/she is taking the preparation seriously.

NOTES

NOTES

5. COLLEGE LIST

Try Some Schools on for Size and Then Find the Perfect Fit

Do you think your college list will only include schools in the Big 10? Do you think your college list will only include schools with a big, brown bear as a team mascot? Do you think your college list will only include schools with a reputation for having the best food in town? We encourage you to answer these questions with a resounding *No!* While we would never turn down a good pizza and we love brown bears, these should not be criteria for choosing a college.

Developing an initial college list should be a holistic process. It is the first step toward finding schools where you will be successful and flourish. If you have started your junior year in high school, now is the ideal time to start your college list.

GET TO KNOW YOURSELF

The first thing you need to do is understand yourself. Be honest and think before you answer the questions below. The goal is to identify schools that are good fits for you. They may not and should not fit your coach's cousin's friend's profile. Your priorities, interests, and strengths are unique to you and will guide you to colleges that you should consider and add to your preliminary college list. This process starts with you being introspective, so here are some questions to think about:

1. **In what type of class do you feel most comfortable and motivated?**
    A. When you are academically at the top—you like to be one of the smarter students.
    B. When you are academically in the middle—you like to be among your academic peers.
    C. When you are academically challenged—you are motivated by others who work hard and succeed academically.

    The answer to this question will help you determine if you will be most comfortable in a reach, target, or safety school. If you chose C, you can certainly apply to all the Ivy League schools, but you still need to ensure that your list is balanced and includes target and safety schools, as well.

2. **How do you prefer to socialize?**
    A. Small gatherings with friends.
    B. Large groups of people where you always see new faces.
    C. Venturing to new places (like the city) with friends.
    D. Cheering on the school's sports teams.

    The answers to this question should get you thinking about what makes you happy socially. If you chose C, then focus on schools located close to a city, with access to music, culture, sports, restaurants, or other things you enjoy.

3. **When are you most comfortable?**
    A. When most people are similar to me.
    B. When there is a mix of people, but still many who are similar to me.
    C. When there are lots of interesting and diverse people around me.

The answer to this question will lead you to examine the demographics of the student body at the schools on your list. If you chose C, you may want to ensure all areas of the country are well represented at the school, along with students from around the globe.

4. **How far are you willing to travel to school?**
    This is a key question. If you want to come home often and easily, then unless you have access to a private jet, perhaps you should consider schools within a 6-hour driving radius from your home. If you choose to look at schools a distance from home, keep in mind the extra cost involved in travel, your ability to handle delays and common travel nuisances, and perhaps most importantly, the inability to come home for a day or two when you are stressed with finals or suffering from a nasty cold.

5. **Will weather play a part in your decision?**
    If you want to join the ski club, perhaps you want to focus on schools in a colder climate. Do you love the beach? Go ahead and find schools in the Sun Belt, but remember your priorities. Distinguish between a *nice to have* criterion and a *must have* criterion.

6. **What do you enjoy learning about? Do you know what you are interested in studying?**
    Most schools offer a wide variety of majors where students can study and explore a variety of subjects. However, if you are confident in your academic path, take a more in-depth look at the majors or colleges within the school. If you are a future engineer, make sure every college on your list has an engineering program and the specific engineering discipline that interests you.

7. **What size college would you consider?**
   A. Very small (under 2,500)
   B. Small (2,500-5,000)
   C. Medium (5,000-15,000)
   D. Large (over 15,000)

The answer to this question should provide a framework for the school environment that is best for you, not a definitive answer. If you chose A, you will identify schools with small class sizes and close relationships with students, teachers, and advisors. If you chose D, these relationships can also be developed, but you will need to put in more effort as you navigate the campus and classes.

GET TO KNOW SOME COLLEGES

Wow! You have now discovered some interesting and new things about yourself! Let's put these valuable insights to work! Open up your computer and get started on some research. There are several search engines that can help you develop a thoughtful college list. College Board, Petersons, and College Niche are a few that can help you identify schools that meet your criteria. This is the first of many times that we will remind you to keep an open mind. Not all the answers above should be weighed equally. Some schools will pop up that offer the city life you want or are the right size, but they may not have the sports spirit you are hoping for. Keep them on the list for now. Remember, you are compiling a list of schools to which you *may* ultimately apply; you are not getting ready for freshman move-in just yet. The list will change as you mature and learn more about yourself and the schools.

Now, what do you do with this long list of schools? It's time to introduce your numbers. Your GPA and standardized test scores are integral components of a balanced college list.

You may not have taken any standardized tests yet, and that's okay. You can still get started with your list and understand how your GPA compares with college profiles. Then, when you have standardized test scores to add, you can update and refine your list. Enter Naviance—your best friend during the college process, perhaps next to the bag of chips and large chocolate bar fueling you as you read this book! Naviance is a software used by most high schools to provide students with college planning tools, and it is going to help you further refine your college list. Login to your Naviance account and familiarize yourself with this software (or its equivalent if your school uses a different tool). Under the *Colleges* tab, you will see *Colleges I'm Thinking About*. Start adding the schools that came up in your searches. Once you have input schools, click on the *Compare Me* button to see how your numbers compare to students at your high school who already applied to the colleges you input. Identify the schools whose academic profiles are similar to yours. These schools should comprise the majority of your college list.

THE PERFECT FIT

Congratulations! You now have an initial college list based on your preferences and your numbers. You have discovered the intangible factors that you are looking for in a college and have matched those with schools whose test scores and GPA are consistent with yours. As you learn more about the schools, stay true to who you are and what you want. Don't worry about the latest college rankings. Don't worry about where your friends are applying. And don't worry about having the perfect list. This is a preliminary list! Schools will come on and off as you move forward in the college admissions process, as your test scores and GPA become finalized, and as your likes and dislikes are further refined.

HOMEWORK FOR THE STUDENT:

- Answer the questions above to discover what makes you happy and start to identify your college preferences.
- Research the schools on your list. Go to the college websites, talk to current students, and talk to your guidance counselor.
- Keep working with Naviance and get acquainted with all aspects of the software and how it can help you with the college admissions process.
- Plan college visits (see *Chapter 6—College Visits*).

HOMEWORK FOR THE PARENT:

- Review your child's college list and understand his/her criteria.
- Have an open discussion about the schools and why he/she has put them on the list.
- Plan college visits (see *Chapter 6—College Visits*).

NOTES

NOTES

6. COLLEGE VISITS

It May Not Be Disney, but Touring Schools Can Be Fun

It may not be a beach vacation on an exotic island. It may not be a ski trip to the snowy Rockies. And it may not be a two-day hike through the picturesque Shenandoah Mountains. But your college visits can certainly be fun, exciting, and deeply meaningful. Visiting colleges is the best way to identify what you like and do not like on a college campus, and this valuable information will help you refine your college list. After your visits, some schools will stay on your college list and some may not. And by considering what you like about the schools you visit, you may discover additional colleges that meet your updated criteria. The following tips will help you make the most out of your college visits.

REVIEW THE SCHOOL CALENDAR

Try to schedule your college visits while schools are in session. You will get the most realistic view of campus life when students are attending classes and are not on break or in the midst of finals. Every college website posts its academic calendar, which includes when students are off for Thanksgiving break, Christmas break, spring break, as well as the schedule for mid-terms and finals. Do your best to plan your visits to avoid these critical dates. Also, consider visiting a cold weather school during the winter to get an accurate picture of what you are in for! We understand that coordination with your busy high school schedule may be difficult and finding the ideal date for a college visit may not always be possible. So, keep in mind that a visit during breaks, such as in the summer, is still better than no visit at all. Perhaps you can visit in the early summer when students may be taking summer session classes or late August when the fall semester has already started. Most school websites also provide a link for admissions events, including information sessions and tours. Be sure to sign up for the events that interest you. This will reserve your place, as well as provide the school with documentation of your intended interest. Demonstrated interest is a topic we will review in our next chapter.

ARRIVE ON CAMPUS

When you arrive on campus, your first stop should be the admissions office. Make sure you have dressed appropriately. It's not a job interview, but ripped jeans and a t-shirt are not your best choice. Be respectful in your attire. Colleges know you are a high school student; just show them you are one who respects education. Introduce yourself and ensure that your name and contact information are correctly noted in their system for your visit. If you are attending an information session, take good notes. Write down the names and emails of anyone speaking, so you can follow up with thank you emails. Write down any programs, classes, activities, or college traditions that are interesting to you. This will help you differentiate between colleges as you move forward in the process, as well as help you write stronger college-specific essays, which may be part of the college's application.

TAKE THE CAMPUS TOUR AND THEN VENTURE OFF ON YOUR OWN

A campus tour should include more than simply listening to your tour guide. Check out the flyers and bulletin boards to see what is happening on campus. Pick up a school newspaper to get a sense of what's important to the student body. Look at places on campus where you'll spend your time if you attend the school—classrooms, labs, business centers, dorms, dining halls, student centers, fitness centers, music rooms, etc. Also, pay attention to the students on campus—are they wearing sweatshirts with the college name and displaying their school pride? Are they congregating on the quad on a beautiful sunny day? Do they seem engaged in the classroom? Are they cheering on the sports teams? Think about what matters to you and how you answered the questions in *Chapter 5—College List*. Do the school and the student body meet your expectations? Have your expectations and college criteria changed after visiting several schools?

TALK TO CURRENT STUDENTS

Talking to students can potentially give you the best information you will get all day. Have lunch in the Student Union. Grab a coffee in the campus café. Walk around campus and pay attention to what you see. Don't be afraid to stop students and talk to them. We have told you not to listen to what your cousin's friend's sister has to say. Now, we want you to walk the campus and listen! Every school has students with varying opinions. Look for patterns. Look for consistencies. Don't be swayed by outliers. We like to start our student conversations with open-ended questions. Here are some suggested questions to help get you started:

- What do you think of it here?
- What are your favorite aspects about this school?
- Is there anything you would change about this school?
- Why did you choose this school and did it live up to your expectations?
- Can you describe student life on campus and off?

Your answers shouldn't come from one person; ask several students. When students like their school, their enthusiasm will be contagious, and they will be happy to talk to you.

KEEP A RECORD OF EVERY VISIT

While your phone should be tucked away and silent during the information session, your camera should be out and active as you walk around campus. As you visit various schools, your memories of them are bound to overlap and blur. Pictures will keep things in focus. Was the student center impressive? Take a picture. Were the labs state of the art? Take a picture. Was the quad filled with students? Take a picture. These pictures will be visual reminders of what you saw and how you felt. Supplement these pictures with notes about each school. You might want to include your overall impressions of the following:

- Location/Town
- Look and Feel of Campus
- Interesting Academic Offerings
- Interesting Extracurricular Activities
- Dorms
- Dining Hall
- Student Center
- Fitness Center
- Classrooms/Lecture Halls

- Interactions with Students
- Overall Positive Thoughts
- Overall Negative Thoughts

DON'T RUSH TO JUDGMENT

Was your visit during a monsoon? Did the car ride take forever? Was your little sister overly annoying? Did you have a hard time connecting with your tour guide? That's unfortunate on all counts, but keep an open mind. None of these factors should influence your thoughts on the school and whether it is a good fit for you. Unless of course, monsoons are a regular occurrence! It's unlikely that every school will meet all of your criteria all of the time and that's okay. At this point, you don't know where you will be accepted, so focus on the positives at each school. Later in the college admissions process, when you hopefully have a stack of acceptances, is the time to look more deeply and analyze and compare the schools that remain on your list. Depending on when you visit, your freshman year of college may be more than a year away, so keep in mind that you and what interests you may change.

FIND YOUR SECOND HOME

Will these college visits make your list of top ten vacations? Probably not, but they can still be fun, as well as provide a chance to spend quality time with your family (even with the annoying little sister). Enjoy this time, while making the most of the trip. The college visit is one of the most important components of the process. Your gut feeling and overall impression of the school is just as important as the tangible aspects and criteria you previously identified. You will be living at college for four years; it needs to feel like home.

HOMEWORK FOR THE STUDENT:

- Identify schools you would like to visit.
- Work with your parents to schedule visits based upon the academic calendar and your family schedule and budget.
- Research points of interest on campus and in the surrounding town/city that should be included on your visits.
- Start a file system to organize the notes and pictures from each visit.
- Research any additional schools for your college list based upon your likes/dislikes from visits.

HOMEWORK FOR THE PARENT:

- Discuss with your child which schools he/she is interested in visiting.
- Work with your child to schedule visits based upon the academic calendar and your family schedule and budget.
- After each visit, get your child's impression of the school before you provide your input.
- Compare notes and have an open discussion about each school.

NOTES

NOTES

7. DEMONSTRATED INTEREST

Show Colleges the Love

Will she say *Yes* to your Promposal? Will he be happy to get your text? Are you looking for a telltale clue that the answer to these questions will be an enthusiastic *Yes*? In many ways, college admissions officers want that same positive indication from you, the applicant. How can you let colleges know that you are interested in them? Unfortunately, flower corsages and smiley-faced emojis won't win over your admissions counselor. However, colleges do need to feel the love, and we will outline exactly how you can accomplish this. You need to show them, as well as tell them, that they are at the top of your college list. This is called demonstrated interest, and it is a critical component of the admissions process. It can set you apart from the competition, and it is often tracked and used by colleges to evaluate candidates.

Why is demonstrated interest so important? Colleges report various statistics involved in the admissions process. How many students applied? What percentage of the applicant pool was accepted? What percentage enrolled as members of the freshman class? These numbers, which are part of each college's public profile, affect college rankings and endowments, as well as directly impact the selectivity rating of a college. High selectivity ratings are prestigious and give colleges bragging rights. And as you can guess, colleges compete for these bragging rights. Therefore, colleges prefer to accept students who they believe are more likely to say *yes* to their offer of admission. So, use this information to your advantage. Show the colleges at the top of your list that, if you are admitted, you are likely to enroll.

APPLY EARLY DECISION

The most obvious way to demonstrate interest is to apply Early Decision. This option is right for you if you are 100% certain about which college you want to attend. The academics are exactly what you are looking for. The social life feels right. You connected with the students you spoke to. The cost of attendance is within your family's budget. You see yourself thriving there for the next four years. Early Decision plans are binding, which means that if accepted, you are committed to attending. So be certain and unwavering. There is no better way to demonstrate interest in a college than to apply Early Decision, but only if you are sure that they are number one!

VISIT COLLEGES ON YOUR LIST

Early Decision plans are not for every student, and there are several other meaningful ways to demonstrate interest in a college. College visits are a great way to show schools that you want to learn more about them and that you care enough to take the time out of your busy schedule to visit their campus. As we mentioned in *Chapter 6—College Visits*, check in with the admissions office when you arrive, as they keep track of which students come to their campus. Visiting the college will provide you with meaningful information about the school and how it fits your criteria, and it is also a key way to let admissions officers know you are interested in their school.

EMAIL YOUR ADMISSIONS REPRESENTATIVE

Emails are another way to demonstrate interest and establish a relationship with your regional admissions representative. Most colleges have a designated admissions officer for your particular state or region. This person is usually the first one to read your application and, therefore, is an important person for you to communicate with throughout the process. A computer search or a phone call to the college can provide you with the name and email address for this contact. Regular communication with admissions is encouraged, but this doesn't have to be a huge time commitment. You should keep in touch, but you don't need to be a stalker! Just remember to take a few opportunities throughout the process to send targeted emails to your admissions representatives. Here are a few possible suggestions:

- **After Your College Visit**. This is the perfect time to introduce yourself and tell the school what you liked about your visit. Be specific and use examples. Make it clear that the email was written just for them. A generic email will not have the same impact as one that highlights specific information.

- **When You Can't Visit, But You Know That You Will Apply to Their College**. Schools recognize that you cannot always visit their campus, so give them another indication that they are important to you. Be direct and tell them why you are interested. Send an email before you apply. Introduce yourself, acknowledge that you are unable to visit, and explain why this college is a good fit for you. Again, be specific and make it clear that the email was written just for them. No one wants a love note with someone else's name scratched off and replaced with theirs!

- **After Submitting Your Application**. This is the ideal time to express your enthusiasm or to tell them about a new achievement. A quick email after applying can communicate your excitement about the possibility of attending the college. Additional information, such as a new leadership position, an honor or award, or a new job should also be sent to admissions. These email correspondences will help differentiate you from other students. You want to be more than a name on a folder; you want to show each school that you are an excited and conscientious applicant with a personal story.

- **If You are Deferred from an Early Decision or Early Action Admission Plan**. This is the time to express your continued interest in the college, and also to reiterate why they should accept you. Reaffirm your commitment to the school, as well as tell them how you will be an active and contributing member of their college community.

Remember as a child being taught about respect and manners? Well, we may sound like your mother when she advised you about how to talk to grandma, but email etiquette is just as important! So, here are a few guidelines. Is your email address *puppiesrule@gmail.com* or *ihatebooks@verizon.net*? Time to retire those accounts and get a new, more professional email account. Or use your school email account. But whichever you chose, make sure that you check all folders associated with that account often and thoroughly.

The emails you send to colleges are reviewed by admissions officers and should be respectful and formal. They should not resemble the casual text messages sent to your friends. Start by addressing the admissions officer as Ms., Mr., or Dr. Do not use their first names unless they have explicitly told you to. Stay away from acronyms or anything found in the Urban Dictionary. Use complete sentences, not phrases. Write words out, do not abbreviate, and do not use texting language. Never substitute *ur* for *your*. Sentences start with an uppercase letter and end with a period. Obvious, right? Not so much. Have someone proof your emails prior to sending them out. An additional set of eyes will always be helpful in catching mistakes. To close our email conversation, let's talk about your name. Even though you are unique, your name might not be. There actually might be another person of the same name applying to college. So, sign every email with your full name, no nicknames or shortened versions, and at least one additional identifier. Identifier examples include the name of your high school, your hometown, or your date of birth.

OPEN EMAILS

Have you received an email from a school on your list? Click on it! Schools often keep track of who opens the mail they send. In addition to it including potentially useful information, this is a simple way to show them that you are interested.

ATTEND COLLEGE EVENTS

Finally, your interest in a college can be demonstrated through your participation in college fairs, high school events, and admissions or alumni interviews. Go to your local college fair. Talk to college representatives, ask questions, take the marketing material home, and leave your name for their records. Is a college representative talking at your school? Go! Dress appropriately, be prepared with questions, and leave your name for their records. Sometimes, colleges will invite you to schedule an interview once they have received your application, but sometimes you must take the initiative and request an interview. If the interview is optional and you are the type of person who is at ease in that type of setting, then sign up for an interview and use this vehicle as another way to show your interest. To determine which colleges offer interviews, go to the schools' websites or call admissions and ask about their interview process.

SHOW YOUR LOVE

Make sure the signs are all there, your interest is obvious, and you show your love! Your date knew you would accept the Promposal. Give colleges that same reassurance that you are an interested, serious, and enthusiastic candidate. Demonstrate your interest with as many of the tips highlighted in this chapter as you can, especially at the schools that mean the most to you.

HOMEWORK FOR THE STUDENT:

- Find the names and email addresses for the regional admissions counselors at the schools on your list.
- Write and proof emails to admissions and ask someone to proofread them prior to sending out.
- Save and organize your emails to admissions representatives.

HOMEWORK FOR THE PARENT:

- Remind your child of the importance of demonstrated interest.
- Review your child's emails before he/she sends them to college admissions representatives.

NOTES

NOTES

8. RECOMMENDATIONS

You Are Impressive— Now Get It in Writing

Grandma thinks you're perfect. Mom thinks you're brilliant. Dad thinks you're totally ingenious. And you're rather proud of your accomplishments, too. While we're confident these accolades are all true, colleges need a more unbiased reference! This is why your guidance counselor and teacher recommendation letters are vital components of the college admissions process. For most college applications, you will need a recommendation letter from your guidance counselor, as well as a letter from one or two teachers.

GUIDANCE COUNSELOR RECOMMENDATIONS

In most high schools, guidance offices are understaffed and overworked. High school counselors need to write recommendation letters for each student applying to college, while, at the same time, focusing on their core responsibilities of helping students with general academic issues. You want your counselor recommendation letter to be notable and personal; you don't want it to sound like every other recommendation that he/she writes. How can you help your guidance counselor write a strong and insightful recommendation letter?

- **Foster the Relationship.** Make it your business to talk to your counselor a few times a year so that he/she can get to know you beyond your transcript. How can you do this? If you are deciding between two classes for next year's schedule, ask your counselor for his/her recommendation. If you are having trouble in a class, ask your counselor for advice. If you are excited to start the college process, keep him/her in the loop with your progress.

- **Complete the Student Brag Sheet or Student Profile.** Every school is different, but most guidance counselors ask you to complete a student profile on Naviance. This form includes questions about your accomplishments, achievements, strengths, weaknesses, and any obstacles you have encountered or overcome. Take your time completing this form and take it seriously. Most counselors use this information as the basis for their recommendation letter. Give specific examples that demonstrate the character traits that you want to be conveyed to college admissions. For instance, if you are a giving and caring person, let your counselor know about your involvement in the local senior home, camp for disadvantaged youth, or cancer awareness fundraiser. If you are a budding entrepreneur, give details about the launch and success of your business. If a family member had an illness that impacted your studies, make your counselor aware of this personal issue so they can include it in the recommendation letter.

TEACHER RECOMMENDATIONS

By spring of your junior year, you should be prepared to ask two teachers for college recommendation letters. One must be in an academic area, and it is preferable if both recommendations are not from the same academic area. For example, try not to ask both your algebra teacher and your geometry teacher for recommendation letters. Do you know what major you want to pursue in college? If so, then consider asking a teacher from that academic area. For example, if you are thinking about a career in medicine, then ask a science teacher. Focus on which teacher knows your strong work ethic and who understands how passionate you are about the subject. It is not necessarily about the class where you got an *A*; it's the class where you demonstrated who you are as a student. Here are some ways you can foster teacher relationships:

- **Go for Extra Help When Needed**. Be prepared with questions and be specific regarding the help you need. This will show your teacher that you have worked through the material as best you can, but now need their help to fully understand the information.
- **Be an Active Class Participant**. Teachers appreciate students who contribute to class discussions and enhance the learning of fellow students.
- **Be Respectful in Class**. Put your phone away and give your teacher your complete attention.
- **Always Complete Assignments**. Submit all assignments on time and make up work that you missed during school absences.

After you have identified which teachers you are going to ask for recommendations, find an appropriate time to ask them. This conversation should be in person and not through email or text message. Be sure to ask them if they need any additional information from you. They might want you to provide a resume, a description of your activities, or a completed questionnaire. Once they agree to write the recommendation, you will need to formalize this request by inputting it into Naviance. This allows the teachers to upload their letters directly to Naviance, which enables guidance to include the letters with your applications. It is your responsibility to track the progress and completion of your letters. Follow up, as appropriate, with your teachers to ensure the letters are completed before the college application deadlines.

ADDITIONAL RECOMMENDATIONS

Do you have a coach who sees your determination? Do you have an employer who recognizes your work ethic and dedication? Have you worked tirelessly for a non-profit organization? If so, you might want to consider asking for an additional letter of recommendation from one of these sources. Not all schools allow for additional recommenders, so check your college list before asking.

BEYOND YOUR NUMBERS

Recommendation letters are an important way for college admissions officers to learn about you beyond your GPA and test scores. Think seriously about who to ask, provide them with any information they request, and always follow-up and thank them for their time and effort.

HOMEWORK FOR THE STUDENT:

- Complete your student brag sheet.
- Develop relationships with your recommenders.
- Request teacher recommendations during the spring of junior year. Enter requests into Naviance.
- Follow-up to ensure recommendations are complete and submitted.

HOMEWORK FOR THE PARENT:

- Review all guidance requirements. Some schools require a parent brag sheet; so, complete these forms, as necessary.
- Discuss with your child the potential options for teacher recommendation letters.
- Follow-up with your child to ensure he/she has requested teacher recommendations by the end of junior year.

NOTES

NOTES

9. MANAGING DEADLINES

Late to Dinner is Fine—
Late to Apply is Not

D id you put the date for your driving test on your calendar? Did you put the date for your friend's Super Bowl party on your calendar? Did you put the date for spring break on your calendar? Of course, you did! You wouldn't want to miss any of these exciting events. The college admissions process is bursting with deadlines that are probably less exciting, but still extremely important, and absolutely need to be tracked and managed. Application deadlines. Testing registration deadlines. Testing submission deadlines. Guidance office deadlines. These critical dates need to be highlighted in your planner, on your desktop, or on your phone. Find the organizational tool that works for you and be diligent in using it to ensure that college admissions milestones and deadlines are met.

APPLICATION DEADLINES

Every school has its own set of application deadlines. These include dates for Early Decision, Early Action, Priority Admission, Rolling Admission, and Regular Decision. *Chapter 11—Applications* will provide details about each of these application options, so review it carefully and make an informed decision regarding which admission plan is best for you at each school on your list.

For now, let's focus on managing the deadlines. First and foremost, the deadlines for each of these admission plans are non-negotiable. They are the dates on which the college must receive your application and supporting materials. It doesn't matter if you have a nasty cold. It doesn't matter if you are on vacation. And it doesn't matter if you are the valedictorian of your senior class. A deadline is a deadline. These deadlines can all be easily found under the admissions tab on the college websites. Stay organized and use whatever tools work for you to keep track of these important dates. Some students like spreadsheets. Some like calendar alerts. Some like bright yellow stickies on their desktop. Know the dates required by your admission plans and work accordingly. While you never want to be the first one at a party, the admissions party works differently. An early submission will send a positive message to admissions that you are motivated, interested, and responsible. Let's break down the process into smaller, more manageable components:

- **Decide How You Are Applying to Each College**. Early Action and Early Decision materials are usually due in November. Regular Decision materials are typically due in December or January.
- **Submit All Applications Before the Required Deadlines**. There are various components to each application, and many are multifaceted and time-consuming. Give yourself plenty of time to work on and review each component.
- **Send Your Standardized Test Scores**. Scores must be sent from the College Board or ACT official websites to each college on your list. This should be done at least two weeks prior to each application deadline.
- **Submit Transcript Request Forms**. Submit these forms to your guidance office for each college on your

list. This should be done at least two weeks prior to each application deadline.

Once you have filled out your forms for guidance, submitted your application, and sent your test reports, take a well-deserved breath and celebrate! But then, prudently track your work. Even though you have sent the required materials, your job is not done. You need to follow up and make sure that each college receives all of the above materials on time. After submitting each component of the application, periodically check each college's application portal to see what their admissions offices have received. Breakdowns in the process have been known to happen. Storms, power outages, and computer glitches can impact the delivery of materials. Missed deadlines are not the fault of your guidance office, College Board, or the ACT website. You are the one applying to college, and it is your responsibility to ensure that your applications are received and complete. If you need to make a repeat request for your transcript, then do it! If you need to resubmit scores, then do it! Check your portals to be sure the schools have what they need to evaluate your application. If your application is not complete, the college will not review it!

TESTING DEADLINES

Standardized tests are generally given once a month throughout the year and registration closes approximately one month before each test date. You can find these dates at *www.collegeboard.org* (for the SAT) and *www.act.org* (for the ACT). As we stated above, you must send your test scores to each school on your list through these websites. Remember that the schools must receive the scores by the appropriate deadlines. While these requests and submissions are electronic, it does not mean there is an immediate transmission of data. Make your requests in advance of all deadlines. As we said, it is your responsibility to make sure colleges receive all supporting material on time.

GUIDANCE DEADLINES

Your guidance counselor will submit your high school transcript and recommendations, but it is your responsibility to make sure that they have everything they need to process your materials. When do they need your brag sheet? When do they need your transcript request form? It is your responsibility to ask and understand the requirements and deadlines for your specific guidance department.

TIMING IS EVERYTHING

Stay organized. Stay current. And stay aware of what needs to be done! Competition in college admissions is tough enough. You don't want to miss an opportunity because you missed a deadline.

HOMEWORK FOR THE STUDENT:

- Decide what tool you will use to keep track of deadlines, including application deadlines, testing deadlines, and guidance deadlines.
- Use this tool and input all of your college deadlines.
- Talk to guidance to confirm their requirements and deadlines.

HOMEWORK FOR THE PARENT:

- Discuss with your child how he/she will manage deadlines.
- Allow your child to manage the process, while staying in the loop and guiding them as necessary.

NOTES

NOTES

10. ESSAYS

You Are Unique—Show, Don't Tell

I am not on social media. I only eat chicken nuggets and pasta. I see everything as a sports analogy. My hair is a wild mess. I sat alone at the lunch table all through middle school. My father was sick throughout my entire childhood.

Everyone has a story. Yours may be funny, quirky, serious or inspiring. But, whatever part of your life you choose to share with college admissions, it needs to be personal, honest and insightful. Tell your story and let it convey or highlight your positive attributes, lessons learned, or obstacles overcome.

THE PERSONAL STATEMENT

Most applications have a main essay that asks you to address a particular question or prompt in the form of a personal statement or essay. This essay is a tool that colleges use to get to know you beyond your transcript and resume. It is your chance to show what makes you unique and what matters to you. Think of it as an interview on paper and use the opportunity wisely! Show your personality and your aspirations. Distinguish yourself from other applicants. After reading your essay, the admissions committee should have a better sense of who you are.

The most effective essays don't try to tell too much, but what they do tell is significant and insightful. Admissions officers read hundreds of essays each year, so yours needs to be memorable and should create a strong visual that welcomes the reader into your world. Allow the reader to smile, laugh, cry, or empathize. Allow him/her to be excited and engaged, and subsequently, become your champion in the admissions process. Admissions officers are the people who accept or deny your application. The more personal your story, the more likely you are to connect with the reader and set yourself apart from the competition.

The two most commonly used college applications are the Common Application and the Coalition for College Access, Affordability and Success. These applications will be explained in more detail in our next chapter. The Common Application personal essay must be between 250 words and 650 words. The Coalition personal essay must be between 300 words and 550 words. The specific questions/prompts vary year-to-year and are found on their websites (*www.commonapp.org* and *www.coalitionforcollegeaccess.org*).

For some students, the perfect topic is clear, and the writing flows. For others, the thought of a long personal essay is scary. If you are in the second group, just take it step-by-step. Start by asking yourself the following questions and writing down your honest thoughts and reactions—even if they seem unimportant. You never know what may spark a great idea!

- What challenges have I faced?
- Have I failed at something that was important to me at the time?
- What risks have I taken?
- Have I stood up for something that was important to me?
- What three characteristics best describe me?
- What makes me smile and laugh?
- What makes me happy and content?
- What makes me most proud?

- Who or what is my inspiration?
- Is there an event in my life that helped shape who I am?
- If my house were on fire, what three items would I save (besides family and pets)?
- What was my most memorable vacation and why?
- How would my friends describe me?
- If I could have dinner with anyone (dead or alive), who would it be and why?
- If I could be anyone for a day, who would it be and why?
- Who is my role model and why?
- Why did I choose my extracurricular activities?
- Where do I see myself in ten years?
- In what ways am I different than my friends?
- What makes me who I am?

Answer as many of these questions as applicable. Add to this list as ideas come to you. But don't delete! Refer back to the essay prompts on occasion and keep adding to your list of thoughts. As you review your responses, you should notice some recurring themes. One of these themes will become the heart of your essay. Getting started on the personal essay is a challenge to many students and finding a topic can be the hardest part. So, write down your thoughts, be open to several topics, and allow yourself plenty of time to brainstorm.

Once you have chosen your topic, it is time to start writing the actual essay. Again, take your time. Your first draft will not be perfect. It may ramble and have spelling mistakes. That's okay. Don't worry about grammar, word choice, or flow; just get your ideas down. Ask yourself these important questions: Is this essay topic working? Am I revealing something about myself to the reader? Is this essay adding to my application? One common mistake that students make is to focus on a coach, teacher, sport, or summer experience. These are all perfectly acceptable topics, but your essay needs to focus on how these people or experiences changed or impacted you. *You* is the keyword. You are applying to college, not your teacher or coach. The goal is for the admissions representative to get to know you through your honest and enlightening personal essay. If you feel you are on the right track, awesome! Keep up the good work and continue to write and revise your work. If your essay isn't coming together as a compelling and insightful piece of writing, then take another look at the prompts and try writing about another topic. Don't be afraid to try several topics. When the writing comes more easily, you have hit upon the right topic.

When your essay is finished, it is important to have someone else read it—for grammar, spelling, and content. Find someone you trust and ask for an honest review. Let them know the role of this essay in the college application process. Remind them that this personal essay is a window into who you are, beyond your GPA and test scores. Accept constructive criticism and continue to revise your essay, as necessary. When you think your essay is ready for submission, take another look at the prompt and make sure you can answer *Yes* to these questions. Did I answer the prompt in its entirety? Did I stay within the word count requirement? Will the reader learn something positive about me? Congratulations! The hardest part is done.

SUPPLEMENTAL ESSAYS

Now, let's move ahead and look at the other writing requirements. Some colleges only require the personal statement you have already completed. But many have additional questions, called supplemental essays. Examples of these school-specific supplements include:

- Why are you applying to this college?
- Why are you interested in this major?
- What is your most meaningful extracurricular activity?

Your answers to these questions should contain information specific to the college you are applying to. Remember the notes you wrote after your college visit? Remember the research you did about each school? Use this detailed information to add substance to your essay. Use this opportunity to show admissions that you want to attend their particular college. Talk about an exciting major, a new science laboratory, their philosophy on community service, the small class size, a specific club or organization, or the engaged student body. Whether you have visited the school or not, show you have done your homework and articulate a concise and meaningful answer to each supplemental essay question.

Exercise some caution with these school-specific essays and do not rush. Are you applying to the University of Wisconsin? Well, they don't want to hear about why you love the University of Michigan. You may be laughing, but we have seen this happen many times. Students try to save time and reuse essays, without careful attention to specifics. It is fine to reuse ideas, but insert school-specific details to make it clear which school you are writing about.

In addition, some schools have optional questions on their applications. If you are interested enough to apply to the school, then find the time and put effort into answering each question on the application. Optional essays are another opportunity to demonstrate your work ethic and high level of interest in the school.

What have we learned about essays? Let's go back to our initial essay examples and provide you with a potential focus for each topic:

I am not on social media. I have developed strong interpersonal skills and a strong sense of self. I do not compare myself to the seemingly picture-perfect world I see online.

I only eat chicken nuggets and pasta. For most of my life, I limited myself in many ways. But recently, I have started stepping out of my comfort zone, and I am learning to branch out with my food choices, as well as in other areas of my life.

I see everything as a sports analogy. My love for sports has taught me the value of each of my teammates, from the leadoff hitter to the pinch hitter.

My hair is a wild mess. I am a timid person; but I strive to be a bit bolder and more spontaneous, just like my crazy curly hair.

I sat alone at the lunch table all through middle school. I discovered I wasn't alone. I worked hard to make meaningful connections and to appreciate the value of friendship.

My father was sick throughout my entire childhood. I didn't have an ordinary childhood, but I learned the importance of health, family, support, and compassion.

FIND YOUR VOICE

Don't be overwhelmed. Find your topic and find your voice. Silly to serious, all subjects can work; it's what you do with them that matters. Be honest. Be insightful. Reveal something about yourself.

HOMEWORK FOR THE STUDENT:

- Brainstorm essay ideas.
- If your topic is not initially evident, answer our questions above.
- Use your notes and research to help you write strong school-specific supplemental essays.
- Have a trusted advisor proofread your essays before submission.

HOMEWORK FOR THE PARENT:

- Offer to work with your child on his/her essays; but remember, it is personal and he/she may choose not to share. Suggest another person that your child can ask for help in proofreading his/her essays.

NOTES

NOTES

11. APPLICATIONS

Keep Breathing—They Don't Have to Be Overwhelming

D o you want to receive a congratulatory acceptance email from your top choice school? Do you want to go to your mailbox and find a big, fat envelope saying, *Welcome to College*? Do you want to open a college portal and be greeted with a fireworks animation? Of course you do! Well, the only way to get a college acceptance is to apply! You have made your college list. You have asked your teachers for recommendations. You have talked to your guidance counselor about their requirements. And you have started to write your college essay. Now it's time to complete the college admissions applications.

The Common Application (Common App) and the Coalition for College Access, Affordability, and Success (Coalition) are both undergraduate admission applications that allow students to apply to multiple colleges and universities using one application. On each of these applications, you have the ability to enter much of your information one time and use it on multiple applications. The Common App and Coalition will save you time and help you stay organized. Some colleges, however, do not use either one of these applications. These colleges have their own school-specific applications, typically found on their websites.

COMMON APPLICATION

More than 750 schools use the Common App. No, you won't be applying to 750 schools, but chances are that you will have several colleges on your list that use the Common App. Excited to start? Ready to lay the groundwork for your college acceptances? Let's walk through the major components of the Common App.

Create Your Account

Go to the Common App website (*www.commonapp.org*) and create an account by providing a valid email address and some basic profile information. As we mentioned earlier, use a professional sounding email address or your school email address—this is not the time to be cute! Take note of the unique identification number that was created for your Common App account. Stay organized and keep this number, along with your username and password, in a file or notebook.

Input Your Personal Information

The Common App is comprised of seven major sections: Profile, Family, Education, Testing, Activities, Writing, and Courses & Grades. Everything that you input into these sections will be provided to each school as you apply.

- **Profile**. This section asks for basic information, including your name, address, contact details, demographics, language preference, and citizenship.
- **Family**. This section is about your parents and siblings. You will need to input where they were born, what they do for a living, and their highest educational level achieved.

- **Education**. In this section, you will provide your high school name, guidance counselor information, any college coursework completed, your cumulative GPA, your senior-year course schedule, a list of your honors, and your career interests.

- **Testing**. This section gives you the opportunity to self-report any of your standardized test scores. This section is optional, and regardless of how you chose to respond, you still need to send official test reports for the SAT, ACT, and/or SAT Subject Tests.

- **Activities**. This section is where you will list and describe your activities—school clubs, athletics, employment, internships, cultural activities, and community service. There is limited space to describe these activities, so complete sentences are not necessary! Use strong action words and concise language to convey what you did and what you achieved. Some words we like to use are: selected, elected, organized, responsible, earned, and achieved. Remember, colleges know what most clubs are, so don't waste your limited space explaining what Make-A-Wish is. Use the space wisely and describe your specific involvement, as well as any impact you had on these organizations.

- **Writing**. In this section, you will highlight the essay prompt you have chosen, and paste your essay into the text box provided. It is best to write and proofread your essay in a word document, and then cut and paste it into the designated area. Remember to stay within the 650-word count limit and directly answer the chosen prompt.

- **Courses & Grades**. This information includes courses and grades as detailed on your high school transcript. Some colleges require this information be completed on the application, while others require only your official transcript from your high school. The Common App will let you know which schools from your college list if any, require this self-reported data. If none of your colleges require this information, this section can be skipped.

Add Your Schools

Use the *College Search* tab on the Common App to search and add colleges to your application. Are you unsure if a school on your list accepts the Common App? Just type the name of the college into the *College Search* section, and if it appears in the drop-down box, then it accepts the Common App. Simply select it and add it to your list. If the college does not appear in this section, then it does not accept the Common App, and you will need to apply to this college using another tool. Continue to search and add colleges until your college list is complete. Your schools will appear, in alphabetical order, in the *My Colleges* tab of the application.

Answer the School-Specific Questions

While the bulk of your information on the Common App is shared with all schools on your list, please note that many schools require additional questions and/or writing supplements specific to them. This information is highlighted under the *My Colleges* tab that we discussed above. Colleges often ask about your intended major or if any of your relatives attended or work for their school. The additional writing requirements are often focused on why you have selected this college, your academic plans, your career plans, or are looking for a more in-depth understanding of an extracurricular activity. Please refer back to *Chapter 10— Essays* for more detail on this subject.

Sign the FERPA Waiver

The final part of the *My Colleges* section includes a FERPA Release Authorization. FERPA stands for Family Educational Rights and Privacy Act. By signing the FERPA, you authorize the release of and waive your right to access specific information. In other words, FERPA states that your recommendation letters will be sent to selected schools, and you waive your right to read or access the information contained in these letters. It is important to sign the FERPA and agree to waive your rights. This signifies to the schools that your recommenders are free to be honest in their assessments of you.

Account Rollover

Do you want to start exploring the Common App before your senior year? Account Rollover allows you to do just that—explore and navigate the application during your junior year. The Common App typically launches on August 1. If you have set up an account before that, then on August 1, it will roll over to the academic year in which you will submit your applications. You can begin answering questions under the *Common App* tab during junior year; these sections will all roll over into your official application. However, not all information will roll over, so wait until August 1 to answer any school-specific questions and essays.

The rollover process is simple. When you come back to complete your application after August 1, there are three key steps you'll need to complete in order to roll over your Common App account:

1. **Initiate.** Sign in using the same email address and password you used to create your account and answer a few quick questions to initiate the rollover process.

2. **Review your College Dashboard**. As the rollover process occurs, you'll be taken to your account *Dashboard*. This is where you'll keep track of all of your application requirements.

3. **Continue to Work on the Common App**. If you worked on any college-specific sections before August 1, you will notice that some answers have not rolled over. Remember questions can change from year to year, so your answers to those questions will not roll over.

Final Steps

Review. Review. Review! The *Review and Submit* button allows you to see a PDF version of your application—exactly what colleges will see—before you actually submit. This is the best way to proof your application. Take your time. You can hit Review and Submit as often as you like to review your applications before you submit them! Ask another person to review your application, as well. When you are confident with the final version, digitally sign and date the form, pay the application fee, and submit!

Yes, the Common App asks for a lot of information! College admissions officers review many applications and do their best to distinguish one student from the next. Therefore, you must do your best to let your application reflect you in the most positive way! Take your time and input your information in stages. Start early, stay organized, and manage your workload as you continue on your college admissions path. It will be worth the ultimate prize of getting accepted to your top choice college!

COALITION FOR COLLEGE ACCESS, AFFORDABILITY, AND SUCCESS

Another application platform available to you is the Coalition for Access, Affordability, and Success. Over 130 colleges and universities accept the Coalition Application, so, like the Common App, it enables you to apply to multiple schools with one application, eliminating the need to input your personal and academic information numerous times. The Coalition platform refers to your specific application as MyCoalition. Let's get started!

Create Your Account

Go to the Coalition website (*www.coalitionforcollegeaccess.org*) and create your account by providing a valid email address and some basic profile information. Again, remember to use a professional sounding email address or your school email address. Take note of the unique identification number that was created for your account. Stay organized and keep this number, along with your username and password in a file or notebook.

Input Your Personal Information

The *Profile* section of MyCoalition is the foundation of your application. You can input as much information into this section as you want, as early as you want. Your profile information will be saved and can be changed at any point as you work through the application process. Everything you input into your Profile will be provided to each college as you apply. Your Profile includes the following pieces of information:

- **Personal Information.** This section will ask you basic personal questions, such as your name, email address, social security number, and the year you intend to start college.

- **Contact Information.** This section will ask you for your address and your home and cell phone numbers.

- **Demographic Information.** This section will ask you about your nationality, the language(s) you know, and what language is spoken in your home.

- **Citizenship Information.** This section will ask about your citizenship status and your birthplace.

- **Family Information.** This section will ask questions about your parents and siblings, including where they were born, what they do for a living, and their highest educational level achieved.

- **High School Information.** In this section, you will provide your high school name and guidance counselor information, along with your cumulative GPA and class rank, if applicable.

- **9th-11th Grade Coursework and 12th Grade Coursework.** In these sections, you will list your high school classes and grades. Have your transcript available to check for accuracy.

- **College Information and College Coursework.** These sections give you the opportunity to report any college coursework or dual-credit courses you have completed.

- **SAT/ACT and Subject Tests.** In these sections, you will add your standardized test information, along with Advanced Placement class information.

- **Financial Aid.** This section notifies the school whether you intend to file for need-based financial aid.

- **Honors & Distinctions.** Here you will list any Honors you have received in the order of importance to you.

- **Academic Interest**. In this section, you can list several academic offerings that you may want to pursue in college.

- **Extracurricular Activities**. In this section, list and describe your activities—school clubs, athletics, employment, internships, cultural activities, and community service. There is limited space to describe these activities, so complete sentences are not necessary! Use strong action words to convey what you did and what you achieved. Some words we like to use are: selected, elected, organized, responsible, earned, and achieved. Remember, colleges know what most clubs are, so don't waste your limited space explaining what Relay For Life is. Use the space wisely and describe your specific involvement, as well as any impact you had on these organizations.

Upload Documents to Your Locker

What is the *Locker*? Unlike your physical locker in school, which probably has forgotten sweatshirts, textbooks, and a sneaker or two, this space is unlimited and organized! The *Locker* component of the Coalition provides private and unlimited digital space in which you can collect and organize important materials (such as documents, test scores, and videos) as a record of your high school experience. Any of the items stored in your *Locker* can easily be submitted to Coalition schools as part of your application. Colleges cannot see what is in your *Locker* without your permission; you choose what you would like to share with each application you submit.

When you're ready to apply to colleges, you can input and track your official high school documents, such as your transcript and recommendation letters in your Locker. First, be sure to add your guidance counselor and teacher recommenders to the *Official Document* section of the *Locker* so that they can upload their parts of the application.

Add Your Schools

Use the *Colleges* tab of the Coalition to search for and add colleges to your application. Are you unsure if a school on your list accepts the Coalition? Just type in the name of the college in the search bar, and if it appears in the drop-down box, then it accepts the Coalition. Simply select it and add it to your list. If the college does not appear below the search bar, then it does not accept the Coalition, and you will need to apply to this college using another tool. Continue to search and add colleges until your college list is complete.

Once your college list is complete, you can view application details and deadlines for your colleges, apply to all your Coalition schools, and keep track of your submission progress, all within the *College* section of the Coalition. Like the Common App, each school may also have some additional school-specific questions for you to answer.

Final Steps

Review. Review. Review! MyCoalition provides you with the opportunity to reach out to trusted adults (by adding their contact information) for their input and to review your applications. It is always advantageous to have several people proof your work before submission. Once reviewed, attach all applicable documents from your *Locker* and you are ready to submit!

SCHOOL-SPECIFIC APPLICATIONS

If you cannot find a school on the Common App or the Coalition, then that school has its own application. School-specific applications can be found on the colleges' websites. Yes, that means there is more information to fill out, but most likely you have done the hard part already. Pull up your Common App and/or Coalition Application and use your responses to completely and consistently fill out these school-specific applications.

TIME TO SUBMIT

Congratulations! By this point, your applications should be complete, and you are one step closer to receiving that coveted congratulatory email from your top college! Just remember to officially send your test scores to each college you are applying to and submit your transcript request forms to your high school guidance office.

HOMEWORK FOR THE STUDENT:

- Stay organized! Keep track of which schools use which applications, as well as which applications you have submitted.
- Be aware of application deadlines.
- Have a trusted advisor proofread your applications before submission.

HOMEWORK FOR THE PARENT:

- Offer to proofread your child's applications or suggest another trusted adult who is willing to do so.
- Remind your child of deadlines to ensure timely submission of applications.

NOTES

NOTES

12. INTERVIEW PREPARATION

Prepare, Practice, and Present Your Best Self

A re you comfortable talking to adults? Do you enjoy talking about your accomplishments? Is your enthusiasm for college contagious? If you answered *Yes* to these questions, then you are the perfect candidate for a college admissions interview. Some schools offer optional interviews as part of the admissions process. If you think an interview will enhance your application, then sign up! Be honest with your self-assessment and, if you do schedule an interview, take the time to prepare and practice.

An interview is an ideal opportunity to demonstrate your interest in a particular college, to highlight and personalize your accomplishments, and to convey what you will add to the college community and student body. Be honest and humble, and let your personality come through, as you talk to the admissions or alumni representative. Thank them for their time and insights and always, always write a personalized thank you note after your interview.

BE YOURSELF AND BE PREPARED

Prepare your answers to these common questions:

- Tell me about yourself.
- Tell me about your family.
- Why do you want to attend our college?
- What can you contribute to our college campus?

- What do you see yourself doing ten years from now?
- Who in your life has most influenced you?
- Tell me the best and worst things about your high school.
- If you could do one thing in high school differently, what would it be?
- Tell me about a time when you displayed leadership.
- Tell me about a time when you displayed responsibility.
- What has prepared you for college?
- What are your greatest strengths and weaknesses?
- Tell me about a mistake you made.
- What is your favorite book?
- What is your favorite subject and why?
- What do you like to do for fun?
- What three adjectives best describe you?
- Do you know what you want to major in and why?
- What are you passionate about?
- What did you do last summer?
- Tell me about a challenge that you overcame.

Prepare your answers to these important questions, but do not recite your responses as if from a script. Practice at home. Get comfortable with giving concise answers. Be prepared with a couple of stories that will illustrate your character, passions, and personality.

At the end of the interview, it will be your turn to ask the questions. Be prepared with several questions for the interviewer. It will show him/her, just as much as confident answers to earlier questions, that you are serious and spent time preparing for the interview. Do not ask questions that are easily found on the college's website. Here are some examples of questions you can ask the interviewer:

- How would you describe the student body?
- What is your favorite part of campus?
- What is the personality of the school?
- Why did you attend this college (for alumni interviewer)?

PUT YOUR BEST FOOT FORWARD

This is your opportunity to stand out, represent yourself in a favorable light, and establish a personal connection with a representative from the school. So, make a good first impression. Sit up straight, look the interviewer in the eye, give a firm handshake, and speak politely, clearly, and confidently. Dress appropriately and respectfully, and ask yourself, *Would Grandma be proud to take me to dinner in what I am wearing?* And as we stated earlier, always follow up with a thank you note that includes specific details discussed during the interview.

HOMEWORK FOR STUDENT:

- Research your colleges' interview policies.
- Sign up for interviews, as appropriate.
- Practice your responses to common interview questions.
- Follow-up with a written thank you note or email.

HOMEWORK FOR PARENT:

- Practice interview skills and questions with your child.
- Proofread the thank you notes he/she writes to the interviewer.

NOTES

NOTES

13. FOLLOW UP AFTER YOU SUBMIT APPLICATIONS

Don't Celebrate Just Yet

You pressed submit! Congratulations on completing this incredible milestone! But before you start celebrating, before you buy that coveted college sweatshirt, and before you catch a serious case of senioritis, take some time to ensure that all components of your application are complete, received by each college to which you are applying, and include your latest accomplishments.

You are almost at the finish line; keep your winning pace going and ask yourself what's left to do. Have you sent your official standardized test score reports to your colleges? Have you asked guidance to send your high school transcript? Are your teacher recommendations on their way? It is your responsibility to ensure that each college has received all components of your application package! Colleges will not review your application unless it is complete. A complete application includes: the application itself (including all writing requirements and payment of fees), test score reports sent from *www.collegeboard.org* and/or *www.act.org*, your high school transcript sent by your guidance office, and your teacher recommendations completed by one or two teachers (that you requested earlier through your high school's Naviance system). Remember to take into account the deadline for each application and manage your action items accordingly.

CHECK YOUR APPLICATION PORTALS

Once you hit submit, most colleges will send you a confirmation email acknowledging receipt of your application. This email will often provide you with a link to their application portal where you will create your personal portal account. The portal is where you can track the receipt and status of your application. Have your test score reports been received and downloaded? Has the college admissions department received your transcript? The answer to these questions and many more will be found in your personal portal. Bookmark this page! Write down your username and password. Check this site often and follow-up until everything has been received. If your portal is missing any check marks, here are some ways to be pro-active and follow-up on the missing items:

- Check with your guidance office to verify they have sent your transcripts and recommendations.
- Log into your collegeboard.org and/or act.org accounts and verify that your test reports have been sent to all of your colleges.
- Review the progress of your teacher recommendations through personal emails or Naviance status updates.
- Confirm your application was sent successfully through the Common App or Coalition sites.

If everything has been sent, but your college has not marked it as received on your portal, call the admissions office at this college. There is often a lag between receipt of your information and when your portal is updated. If needed, resend any or all components that are missing from your application package. Remember, this is your responsibility! So, pay attention to your deadlines and resend any application components on a timely basis!

YOU ARE ALMOST DONE

If you followed these steps, your college applications will be complete and ready for review by the colleges! This, however, is not the end of your communication with the admissions representatives. Hopefully, you established a nice connection with them through the admissions process, as we outlined in *Chapter 7—Demonstrated Interest*. It's time to keep building on this relationship and your applications by sharing any new accomplishments with them. Were you just inducted into National Honor Society? Did you get a new job? Did you recently receive an award for your community service achievements? By sharing accomplishments that occurred after you applied, you are exhibiting your continued motivation and work ethic, along with bolstering the merit of your application.

HOMEWORK FOR STUDENT:

- Check your college portals and review the completeness of your applications.
- Take all appropriate actions and adhere to deadlines to ensure colleges receive all components of your application.

HOMEWORK FOR PARENT:

- Encourage your child to stay organized and write down all usernames and passwords for each college portal.
- Remind your child to check his/her portal on a regular basis until each application is complete.

NOTES

NOTES

14. AFTER YOUR ACCEPTANCES ARRIVE

Now You Can Celebrate

Are acceptance letters piled high on your desk? Okay, are they scattered all over your bedroom floor? Do you proudly wear t-shirts and sweatshirts from the colleges that accepted you? Congratulations! Now it's time to choose which path you will take, which shirt you will wear, and which college fits you best.

MAKE AN INFORMED DECISION

Take your time making a decision. Most colleges have a May 1st deadline for you to accept or deny their offer of admission, so think carefully about the different facets of college life before sending that enrollment deposit! Here are some useful tips to help you make your final decision.

Compile Your List and Ask/Answer Critical Questions:

- Did you visit the colleges you are considering? If not, now is the time!
- Does the college offer the major(s) in which you are most interested?
- What is the process to declare a major? Is it competitive?
- What is the personality of the student body?
- What do students do outside of the classroom?
- Can you afford the college (considering financial aid and/or merit scholarships that you were offered)?

PARTICIPATE IN ACCEPTED STUDENTS DAY ON THE COLLEGE CAMPUS

If possible, visit the colleges that interest you the most. Talk to current students. Attend a class or two. Talk to admissions representatives. Ask specific questions. Listen to what your gut is telling you. Are you excited? Do you feel comfortable? Trust your instincts. In this situation, the intangibles are just as important as the tangible qualities of a college.

COMPARE YOUR CHOICES

Identify the criteria that are most important to you. Do you absolutely want a school that offers a degree in Mechanical Engineering? Do you want to be within driving distance of home? Do you prefer warm weather? It is highly unlikely that a college will meet all of your criteria. Do not compromise on your dream of becoming an engineer. If flying to and from school will present a financial hardship, then only consider the schools closer to home. And now to the weather. This is most likely a preference, not a necessity. You can always get some snow boots and a warm coat!

EVALUATE YOUR FINANCIAL SITUATION

Include your parents in an honest and open conversation regarding finances. Compare financial packages—including financial aid and merit money—awarded to you. Understand your financial exposure for each college on your final list. Are you prepared to work while in college? Will you need to take out student loans? Finances are important; take this discussion seriously.

DECISION DAY

Carefully read the directions for your top choice college's enrollment procedures. Sign any necessary documents and send in your deposit. Then proudly wear that sweatshirt on May 1!

INFORM COLLEGES OF YOUR DECISION

Be respectful of the admissions process and email the colleges whose offers of admission you are declining. Other students may be hoping for a waitlist acceptance, so alert the colleges that you are turning down and give up your spot in their freshman class.

THANK COUNSELORS AND TEACHERS

Let your guidance counselors and teachers know your great news! Thank them for their letters of recommendation, insights, and support during this stressful, but very rewarding time in your life!

TIME TO BREATHE!

You did it! You applied, you were accepted, and you made an informed and exciting decision. Enjoy the end of senior year and make the most of your time at home. Start thinking about roommates and what you need for your new room. Explore your college's website and course offerings. And when it is time to start packing, see Appendix B for a college packing list. Congratulations on completing this journey! Best of luck as you embark on your next path! And **NO HOMEWORK!** At least until September, when you will officially be a college freshman!

APPENDIX A

DEFINITION OF COMMON TERMS

What Does It Mean?

APPLICATION AND ADMISSION TERMS

Acceptance: The decision by an admissions department to offer enrollment to a student.

Coalition Application for College Access, Affordability, and Success: An undergraduate admission application that allow students to apply to multiple colleges and universities using one application.

Common Application: An undergraduate admission application that allow students to apply to multiple colleges and universities using one application.

Deferred Admission: A category of admission used in conjunction with early plans (Early Action or Early Decision) to indicate that a student has not been admitted early, but will remain in the applicant pool for reconsideration during the review of Regular Decision applications.

Deferred Enrollment: This is a category of admission available at some institutions for fully accepted students who wish—for a justifiable reason—to take a semester or year off before enrolling in college.

Denial: The decision by an admissions department not to offer a student admission to a particular institution.

Early Action (EA): When a prospective student applies for admission by an early deadline (before the Regular Decision deadline) and receives notice of acceptance, denial, or deferment. There is no obligation to enroll if accepted under Early Action.

Early Decision (ED): Similar to Early Action, under the Early Decision plan, students apply to an institution early in senior year and receive early notification of admission. However, unlike Early Action, if accepted under the Early Decision plan, students are obligated to attend the institution. Early Decision students and their guidance counselors sign a contract with the college at the time of application to acknowledge that they understand the obligation to attend if accepted. Some colleges and universities offer both ED and EA options, so read the college admission requirements carefully to make sure you know what you're applying for.

Notification Date: The date by which applicants who are accepted for admission are expected to notify the institutions of their intent to enroll and make enrollment deposits. That date is often on or around May 1st.

Rolling Admissions: This is a practice used by some institutions to review and complete applications as they arrive, rather than according to a set deadline.

Single Choice Early Action: SCEA is when a prospective student applies for admission by an early deadline (before the Regular Decision deadline) and does not apply early to any other schools (either through Early Decision or Early Action). Students may still apply to other institutions that have Rolling and/or Regular Decision processes. SCEA applicants may also apply to a public institution under an early plan, provided an early application is required for consideration for merit scholarships and/or special programs.

Waitlist: An applicant is put on the waitlist when an admissions officer or committee decides to offer the applicant the opportunity to enroll in the institution only if there is space available in the incoming class after fully admitted students have responded to their offers to enroll. This category of admissions is reserved for students whose profiles are strong, but who are marginally qualified in comparison to the overall strength of others in the pool of applicants.

TESTING TERMS

ACT: An alternative to the SAT, this test is widely accepted by a broad range of institutions and is administered throughout the school year. The ACT assesses English, mathematics, reading, and science reasoning, and these scores can be used in lieu of SAT Subject Tests. There is also an optional writing test that assesses students' skills in writing an essay. The ACT is scored on a scale of 1 to 36 for each of the four areas. The four subject area scores are averaged to create a Composite Score. Check with the schools you're interested in to see if ACT scores are part of their college admission requirements.

PSAT/National Merit Scholarship Qualifying Test: Known as the Practice SAT and similar in format to the SAT, this test is usually taken in October of junior year; but it is shorter and takes less time than the SAT. It is a qualifying instrument for the National Merit Scholarship Awards Program and can be helpful for early college guidance.

SAT: This is a widely used college entrance examination. The SAT measures verbal and mathematical skills. Students may earn a total of up to 1600 points on the exam (up to 800 points in each of the exam's content areas: Math and Evidenced-Based Reading and Writing).

SAT Subject Test: SAT Subject Tests (also known as SAT 2 tests) are offered in many areas of study including English, mathematics, many sciences, history, and foreign languages. Some colleges require students to take one or more SAT Subject Tests when they apply for admission.

Score Choice: Score choice allows the test taker to decide which SAT scores to release to prospective colleges.

MISCELLANEOUS COLLEGE TERMS

Demonstrated Interest: This includes a student's expression of his or her desire to attend a particular college. Demonstrated interest includes campus visits, contact with admissions officers, and other actions that attract the attention of college admissions personnel. While not all institutions use this as a factor in accepting students for admissions, studies have shown that more than half of schools do consider demonstrated interest in their admissions decisions.

GPA (Grade Point Average): Quantitative measure of a student's grades. The GPA is calculated by averaging the numerical value of a student's grades. It is cumulative, starting freshman year.

Reach School: A college or university that a student has a chance of getting into, but the student's test scores, GPA and/or class rank are on the low side compared to the school's profile. The top U.S. colleges and universities should always be considered reach schools.

Recommendations: Statements or letters of endorsement written on a student's behalf during the college application process.

Safety School: A college or university where a student is likely to gain admission because he/she clearly meets the admission requirements. It's important, though, that the school also be one that the student would want to attend, should he/she not gain admission to more selective colleges.

School Profile: This is an overview of a high school's program, grading system, course offerings, and other features that the school submits to admissions offices. Admissions offices use this information to compare students' GPAs with the academic reputation of their high schools.

Selectivity: Selectivity is the degree to which a college or university admits or denies admission based on the individual student's record of academic achievement. In general, a highly selective school admits 25% of applicants, a very selective school admits 26% to 49% of applicants, a selective school admits 50% to 75% of applicants, and a school with open admission admits applicants based on space availability.

Target School: A target school is one where a student meets or surpasses a college's average stats. Students are likely to be accepted by target schools, but it is not a sure thing. Most students end up attending target schools, so they are an important part of every college list.

Waiver to View Recommendations: Also known as FERPA, this is a form on which students agree to waive their right to review recommendation letters before they are sent to the colleges or universities.

Yield: This is the percentage of accepted students who actually enroll in a college or university freshman class.

APPENDIX B

A COLLEGE PACKING LIST

Grab Your Coupons—It's Shopping Time!

BEDDING
2 Sheet Sets (Twin Extra Long)
2 Pillow Protectors
2 Pillow Cases
Mattress Bed Bug Protector
Mattress Pad
Foam Mattress Topper
Pillow
Comforter
Blanket
Bed Risers

BATH
Large Towels
Hand Towels
Washcloths
Shower Caddy
Toiletries and Medications
Flip Flops (Shower Shoes)

STORAGE/ORGANIZE
Under Bed Storage Containers/Drawers
Over-the-Door Hooks
Hangers
Double Hanging Closet Rod (for kids with lots to hang)

Backpack
Drawstring Gym Bag
Overnight Bag
Command Strips (variety of sizes)

LAUNDRY
Laundry Bag/Hamper
Laundry Detergent
Color Catcher (for when you mix lights and darks—and you will)
Clorox Wipes for Room
Tide-to-Go Stick

ROOM APPLIANCES
Laptop
Printer/Ink/Cables
Desk or Night Table Lamp & Light Bulbs
Cell Phone/Charger
Clock
Surge Protectors
Flashlight/Batteries
Extension Cords
Dust Buster (for cleaning—yes, you will need to clean)

ROOM FURNISHINGS
Rug
Tapestry/Wall Decorations
Photographs/Photo Collages
Over the Door Mirror
Dry Erase Board
Command Strips
Wastebasket
Garbage Bags
Refrigerator/Microwave

DESK SUPPLIES

Notebooks
Folders
Computer Paper
Pens/Pencils/Sharpies/Highlighters
Stapler/Staples
Tape
Pencil Sharpener
Calculator
Scissors
Paper Clips
Sticky Notes
Flash Drives

KITCHEN SUPPLIES/SNACKS

Water Bottles
Snacks
Coffee Machine

OTHER

Umbrella
Health Insurance Card
Tool Kit for Moving In (everything needs to be assembled, and it's never easy!)

NOTES

NOTES

NOTES

NOTES

NOTES